This book was painted by
hand digitally, with no use of AI.
www.aaronmstudios.com
ISBN/SKU:979-8-218-56926-6

This Book Belongs To:

____

I Love My Body From Head To Toe

by Danielle Raspberry Levin

illustrated by Aaron McKissen

I love my body from head to toe.

I love my body as it does grow!

I love my wiggly toes.

I love my smelling nose!

I love my eyes, they help me see.

My eyes are special,
just like me!

Also amazing are my ears.

They can hear both far and near!

My mouth and teeth are pretty neat.

I like my tongue that tastes things sweet!

I like my hands
that wave “hello”.

My fingers zip up my jacket
when it's time to go!

My elbows and knees and joints all bend.

My arms hold lots of hugs to lend!

I love my neck

and my stomach too.

On each foot I put a shoe!

My front and back and sides are great.

My legs are used to help me skate!

Sometimes we scrape or break a part or two.

Most often those parts are healed
for me and you!

I am thankful for each body part.

We are all blessed right from the start!

I love my body from head to toe.

All bodies are beautiful as they grow!

The End

Dedication: This book is dedicated to EVERYBODY!

Gratitude and Appreciation: We would like to thank EVERYBODY!

Danielle Raspberry Levin is a writer and poet who has won an honorarium for her writing in the biopsychological health field, written greeting cards, newspaper articles, and has appeared on a television gameshow.

Aaron McKissen is an illustrator and cartoonist who works on TV commercials, storyboards, graphic design, and lives in Colorado.

www.ingramcontent.com/pod-product-compliance
Lightning Source LLC
Chambersburg PA
CBHW042122110726
48006CB00002B/726

9798218569266